to see the queen

THE LEXI RUDNITSKY FIRST BOOK PRIZE IN POETRY

The Lexi Rudnitsky First Book Prize in Poetry is a collaboration between Persea Books and The Lexi Rudnitsky Poetry Project. It sponsors the annual publication of a poetry collection by an American woman who has yet to publish a full-length book of poems. Lexi Rudnitsky (1972–2005) grew up outside of Boston. She studied at Brown University and Columbia University, where she wrote poetry and cultivated a profound relationship with a lineage of women poets that extends from Muriel Rukeyser to Heather McHugh. Her own poems exhibit both a playful love of language and a fierce conscience. Her writing appeared in *The Antioch Review, Columbia: A Journal of Literature and Art, The Nation, The New Yorker, The Paris Review, Pequod,* and *The Western Humanities Review.* In 2004, she won the Milton Kessler Memorial Prize for Poetry from Harpur Palate. Lexi died suddenly in 2005, just months after the birth of her first child and the acceptance for publication of her first book of poems, *A Doorless Knocking into Night* (Mid-List Press, 2006). The Lexi Rudnitsky First Book Prize in Poetry was founded to memorialize her and to promote the type of poet and poetry in which she so spiritedly believed.

Winners of the Lexi Rudnitsky First Book Prize in Poetry:
2012 Allison Seay, *To See the Queen*
2011 Laura Cronk, *Having Been an Accomplice*
2010 Cynthia Marie Hoffman, *Sightseer*
2009 Alexandra Teague, *Mortal Geography*
2008 Tara Bray, *Mistaken for Song*
2007 Anne Shaw, *Undertow*
2006 Alena Hairston, *The Logan Topographies*

to see the queen

•

Allison Seay

Winner of the 2012 Lexi Rudnitsky First Book Prize in Poetry

A Karen & Michael Braziller Book
PERSEA BOOKS / NEW YORK

Persea Books, Inc.
277 Broadway
New York, NY 10007

Library of Congress Cataloging-in-Publication Data
Seay, Allison, 1980–
[Poems. Selections]
To See the Queen / Allison Seay. — First edition.
       pages cm.
"Winner of the 2012 Lexi Rudnitsky First Book Prize in Poetry."
Poems.
ISBN 978-0-89255-423-2 (original trade paperback : alk. paper)
I. Title.

PS3619.E259T67 2013
811'.6—dc23

                        2012047440

First edition
Printed in the United States of America
Designed by Rita Lascaro

for Luke

to see the queen

contents

liliana

THE FIGMENT

If I am still enough I see Liliana, a figment.
I try to tell her about sadness. I try
to be specific; I say, "God

is abusive." I say, "When my lover said
he no longer loved me
I felt I was covered in ropes."

But then she vanishes,
as God does, or she returns in a different form—
this time as an avalanche, a ledge of snow, slipping ''

from the roof of a warehouse into
even more snow. I will tell her next I think
that is one way of living: slipping off— *resbalando*

into some indistinguishable state
of more and more snow.

HER HAIR, BEFORE IT IS PINNED

There was rhubarb jam in the morning
and every evening. Also a bowl of cherries.
That was my youth, when Liliana was beginning.

That was before I let a man wreck me,
or let a woman touch me. Before I knew
how a jaw could grow fierce and how suddenly.

Before I thought of the sun as explosion, dusk as death.
No one I knew had killed themselves or tried to.
I had not yet wanted to die.

I did not know how to talk about art. I did not know
the difference in need and want. I did not believe in God.

I was never hungry.
I was not afraid as I am now afraid.

4

THE QUEEN

The figment *producto* is the same as the sadness sometimes.

Wild gold and dark red. The color of snow under a streetlamp.
Or of smoke pluming from a house
under a white sky in the morning. The color

of a queen. I try to keep her, even while she is leaving
and even after I know she has left. I shout,
"Are you there, are you even there?" meaning God

but also Liliana. I want to ask her
which is worse: dying *moribundo*
or being dead. And then I can see her floating away
estar muerto

as down a hill of ice. With her she has one half
of my whole being. She holds me high above her head
and I wave to myself like a flag.

THE SADNESS

Other times the figment is God. We discuss choices
that would leave me not unhappy, keep the darkness

in the near-distance. But then when I am
on the brink, God becomes a crystal song, a hymn

in the piano's high octaves. Or God is the smell
of apple soap in the morning rooms or the feel

of sun on a horse's back, pure and kind.
He enters the strange field of my mind

the way, after a long day of silence, the voice trembles
in the throat and enters the air, like a shy animal.

When I look at myself in a mirror, there is no answer.
In one eye, God lives with me. In the other,

there is the bright loud world below,
my figure on the sill of a window.

GOD'S WOODS

The worst part of seeing figments
is not seeing them.

My life is not so hard except for that—alone

in a world which moves around me as a silent film, or is
too far away to touch, or is as a fantasy. I am as distant

to myself as someone I read about

which is to say the worst part
of knowing I exist is not knowing

whether I am or am not a figment.

LILIANA IN AIR

It was for a moment ruthless,
the aloneness, when, though I was only briefly abandoned,
when
the white sun was hidden, undone, but there
anyway there
the shadow I was tracing of hers
vanished in the grass (death of a queen)
and I felt as a gasp the foolishness
of love, of keeping her as a body
knowing how quickly we appear
and disappear and the difference in her being
and not being had been but air and cloud.

8

THE FEVER

The winter that kept my fever all season
was the winter I saw the neighbor girl's body
being taken from the house.
And who would have trusted
me murmuring in my sleep?
Who could know I felt I was drowning?
Who knew the sea-fear, the airlessness?

And she was with me as a figment
in my fever-haze: she *was* the fever;
she was the ocean, the ocean
I felt moving inside me all winter,
the ocean into which they threw our bodies
because (they thought)
it was what we wanted.

THE SISTERS' INCIDENT WITH THE FIGMENT AT THE BUS STOP, 1985

for Emily

We were only girls then
and we did not yet not love ourselves.
Our deaths were only beginning to ripen.

In one dream of us, I wait for her the way, once,
I did not. I help collect her spilled lunch
from the gravel. We miss the rumbling bus and spend

all day hiding in the neighbor's wild yard
and walk to an almost-dry creek and do not talk
about the many little deaths inside of it.

In that dream, there is not her red frightened face
outside the glass. I did not abandon her. The apple
is not rolling in the street because this time

I saved it. In that one, the future
sits between us like a figment in the grass
and says we have time still to decide our lives.

We make for her a jewelry of clover
and we let her be the queen.

LATE APOLOGY

The bees came by the hundreds
and by the hundreds was she stung,

their little shell-bodies working like a net.

And when I saw her dead in the creek
(bee queen of my dream)

it was the first time I feared being found
face down dead like a coward.

UNEVEN LOVE

How to lie was something learned.
It meant love
at the time anyway.

Mine will be a long life
feeling always a little ruined,
deep in a well,

knowing the worst thing
I am capable of
not telling. Once did I see the figment as a man.

One man in particular
and the most unusual I have known.
I knew him in a different city.

He was older but not old
and I lied to save us (him)
from disgrace. He said even

without love there is a story of love.
Even without sex, desire.
It does not matter; I understand the strange logic

by which we lived:
to withhold the truth meant
we could create a new one,

a separate thing
true or not un-true.
It was our arrangement.

LILIANA, THE LION

The crisis in bloom is not solvable in a day, or from one room.
A thing impossibly tame, Liliana is as an animal calmed,
her hair in knots, her eyes closed.
And I am a child again, silent and sad
in the rocking chair not rocking, the figment and me not talking.
There are the morning sounds: gulls, an egret, hushing sea oats.
She worries a coin in her hand and then dismisses
whichever wish I might have had
into the marshland below.

BATHING

I have been alone with the thing itself.
The depression. The defective heart. God.

Inside my mind it is dawn. A wolf appears with a bird
in its mouth. Blue feathers, my fate, the beautiful white throat.

THE DIFFICULT WAY

The difficult way is mouthful by little mouthful
soft soft loud a string
of sweet autumnal days and then a Day
of nothingness only numb gray brimming
hours upon hours etcetera etcetera
when it feels people are standing closer
to me than I am standing to them
what do they all do
the people
when they are alone with their lives

I wish I could arrange the disturbances
of my life one mouthful of things to think about
and another of things not to
the foolish from the grave the jealousy
from the love arrange things
as though one did not have to be disturbed
if one wished not to be
to swallow the difficulty or not

When I go to the end of the road
it tastes like aloneness in my mouth
(sour thirsty thick iron someone else's smoke)
and there is nothing in the box and I come
back inside and smooth the newel post and rest
on the last stair
and this is what it is like to wait for and not get
the letter no sign from you

LILIANA IN THE HIGH GRASS

I tell her not to go.
I explain about the missing.

Like an empty room. Or the room
with only a mattress on the floor.

No mirror. No bureau and no chair.

Empty as bath water
without the body.

A lamp without a bulb, Liliana
without shade.

Hunger after the fever. I want,
I want, I want.

To miss her is as the mute in terror,
shrieking without sound.

The missing is most as I lie all day alone
in the high grass on a white sheet

long enough that when I rise
there is a second body of me

left like an effigy in the dark yard.

It is not permanent. It is she.
And then we disappear again.

SLOW NIGHT SHOW

All season I went sunbathing beside the pear tree.
The sun was a hazy halo and the world was green and calm.

I did not speak much then, even when I should have—
not when she came with a spade and made in the field

a measured hole heart-deep and so long she could lie down
or almost. Not by dark when it was a grave larger than a
    woman's.

I thought I could see the silence, ticking, and almost said
(to no one), *what do we have here?* but did not speak.

It was she who buried—shoveling the dark—
whatever it was I wanted to know.

NIGHT WITHOUT MUSIC

Sometimes I try to be her altogether
even if she is but a figment

I like to see her dark hair
pool around her I like
to hear her voice like a rumor

and when she is not near
the room darkens
the world is winter-killed

when I am alone
there is nothing
to help the silence of myself

no not one
hundred pianos

SICK ROOM

It is too simple to say the figment is inside me or is myself,
or whichever of my selves, in some thick air.
Or even to say the figment is an illness.

Or that is why I took to the upstairs room
with the green lamp and the brass chain,
room with a music box, room with the cage but no rabbit.

I heard the people in my house say about the fevers—
that my body was like a house on fire.
And I remember the white curtains white as the sun.

That is when I became a different kind of being, a figure
in the sheets with a vision
of kerosene. And though there was no one to tell,

I saw her, Liliana with her long hair,
each day, just before the blinds were drawn.

geography of god's undoing

HOUSE FIRE

There she is with a house in her eyes,
or what is left of it, the house no longer a house.

And here is the fire that looks like a mouth
that is trying to swallow too much—

this town, a season, the sky,
a girl in her dry lace gown.

And here are the birds, circling her,
she who remembered too late

the kerosene lamp, she who thinks the birds
know the truth: *it was you, it was you,*

they caw. And here are the snakes
she did not know were underneath, more vulgar

now that they're dead, the fangs charred open.

At night, she sits in the soot
until she remembers quick as a flame: snake

husks everywhere. The snakes, the *snakes*—
there is no telling which ashes are theirs.

RUNAWAY BRIDE

Before they fell they waved like flags, the leaves,
and as they broke, there became a lovely order

to the dying.
                         The water spider moved
in no hurry at the bottom of the drained pond.

Everything seemed as it should.
                                         Because I could
I even spent a while throwing apples

at a fence post. Over and over, my arm hurled
the poor things farther and farther

from the tree that had released them.

MY HUSBAND, THE ROE

Before the joy there was the end before the end
the ugliest before the worst before I said no
before he asked me to marry him before
I wanted him to ask me before he loved me at all
before he knew I moved to town before I moved to town
I had to move before I had nothing
before there was nothing left or nothing left to lose
before I had everything to lose before
the fire and after before
I thought of women and men before I knew
I was a woman before I was raised a doll
before I knew my name before
I had a name before I was born
he was born already

TOWN OF UNSPEAKABLE THINGS

Then there was the time I looked directly into the face
of the life I thought I was missing,

of love. I used to think to be not alone meant
never having to walk through the high wheat

or struggle in the water. Not having to decide not
to fling from some height.

Once, the two of us rode one bicycle.
I wore a straw hat and perched on the handlebars

and beside us the sea oats swayed like skirts
and I heard a trilling in the crabgrass.

The sidewalks were bleached as grecian stone
as we rode past the fish shop smelling of morning—
salt, bread, limes, men.

Riding in front, it was such that
I could not be heard always, at least not the first time

for you pedaled into the wind
and my hair was a ribbon in your eyes.

I said I thought bougainvillea was a stoic plant
and then had to say twice, *No, stoic!* and then
No, the bougainvillea! and then you said easily

it was nothing like that at all.

But our future was clear enough when I asked if you saw
the clean aprons of those men

(*How much longer you think until they clean the fish?*
Did you see how white those aprons were? Did you see?)

To which you said
How much is it, then, you think you need?

ONE MAN TOWN

A man asked me to marry him.
It was a day cloud-scarce, the sky bright and skeletal
like a beginning. I saw right through

to his wild green heart
as he explained the impossible, believing
if there is a time machine it is not a ship in space,

but a horse on the hemline of a field
fearless in one direction, toward sunup.
Then, the night sky would bloom

into brilliance and *there*, see?, there I am—he can
barely make me out—a figment tearing toward him
through the spring, at last.

TOWN OF THE BELOVED

We rested on a blanket by the water
where I combed the sand and spoke your name gently

You slept but I was not tired and never have I studied
the fullness of a back not even of the dying

propped on their sides as I did yours then

I tried to mimic your breathing though I did not close my eyes
at least not for long instead I kept a kind of vigil

swatting for you what seemed a thousand nameless insects

See it was afternoon the ocean warm to boredom
boat oil and pelicans and I thumbed through a book

while I waited for you to stir to apologize but for what
for disappearing for leaving me to distinguish alone

my desires to want you or want to become you

Wake up please wake so that I might tell how it is
I can for you sit all day in a field of sand

ULTIMA THULE

the leaves move across the sky like sparrows
the sparrows fly across the field
the field is a wasteland
the wind chimes chime in the windy eaves
the air is a chime
the town smells of diesel and grass
the grass hides the snakes
the snakes
the coil
my life only uncoils or recoils
one bird flies at the window
the broken glass
the whole room
half our bed a sheet of tiny prisms
we sleep like that
you will not learn
again your truck is out of gas
again nowhere
my hair to my waist once
and then to my chin
I thought I was saving you
and the stray cat
and the fire in the kitchen
at the end
the end of the known
the borders
the refusal of love
the fine enough
the answer is there is no answer

WOLF TOWN

Apparently there was a place away from here
that would save us—except he went alone,
to paint and drink and tear down and rebuild.
Some time, though, we would live there
which was among other things supposed:
the green sash on the dress, the orchids,

the fathers toasting our lives, our lives.
And it may take forever to finish imagining
the shutters, the rooms, the flowers and vines.
What was that story of a beam in the ceiling
that took him weeks? My whole life is in and out
of the kitchen: either the door opened to the woods
so we faced the bright world or, while we ate that
little supper, we kept our backs to the wolves.

TOWN OF THE EARLY MARRIAGE

I have not yet reconciled the places we have been,
or how we could argue quietly but with contempt

(even while watching turtles sun or tossing petals in a current).

Once in a park I loved you down as a whore
and if they saw us then the people ignored.
But every man I see now is a man somehow you. The man

hauling hay, or by the hedges holding shears; man
on a ladder toward the roof; half a man's form working
on an automobile; man chopping wood; man slogging

through gravel with a wagon, swatting a fly;
man in the dust, savage with beauty.

The mystery of us is still unsolved; the sun
is always aslant. I think often
of how we walked the field: even happy,

you kept an axe-length's distance from me.

TOWN OF LONGING

the cicadas loud inside and out the trees
darkness against a lesser dark sky
there is a melancholy band practicing
three houses down playing one song all night
all the lowly lit bungalows looking drowsy
the dogs and a cloud of cats
the maples ablaze one leaf at a time
and no one ever sure of anything
any given night
clink of bottles or porch door slap
sometimes a different voice or curbed car
something other than what we are used to
in my case for example for a few days
they may have heard a man's low moan
from my open window and wondered
who before had we not noticed
what in the world is she doing
who is that man who comes before dawn
and leaves in the afternoon
but we were our own time own sound
until that was quieted too
and things resumed and fall came usually
and still I am as unsure as the rest of them
I never understand how to figure
one routine then another then another
accreted over time continuous
until it is life itself
in other words the beauty

TOWN OF MY FAREWELL

I was reading in a field by some tracks.
One train passed and shattered the enormous silence.
Then its departure made the emptiness greater.
A fox ran over the still-trembling rails. And one crow circled.
And the ivy unfolded like wings.
There was thistle and lilac. And every direction I faced
there was more and more I thought I would have to leave.
Another dragonfly. Another thing in bloom. The silence was
a kind of nothingness brimming. It was as when
we shared a house
and moved in and out of filled rooms trying
to leave one another. There is always so much to consider.

TOWN OF SMALL FIELDS

What I want to describe for you
is the nest I found fallen among the wineberries.
And the sparrows that flew through the bean fields.
The one I decided to name for you.
And, as I was walking, how I remembered you
in the early morning: at the window with your coffee
and fruit, the red-checked tablecloth.
And how I understood for that moment
the story of how we came together
and tore apart. How I began to feel it in the dark.
How whatever was between us
had worn thin as the nest threads, until
what had once been how we lived
had unraveled as marvelously as it had been made:
thing by small thing, hour by hour,
mostly without witness.

DEVIL TOWN

They covered the catastrophe in the usual ways.
The lips were cemented and he was strange-colored—
mango bark or wheat. His hands had been placed
over his stomach. No one could tell the bullet
entered there and so no one spoke of it. One woman
went up close to him and said, "Oh God, oh
God," and then she ran to a patio.
I could not hear what else but through the glass
I saw her look skyward and shake out her hair
so that it flew behind her as a cape.
A blackbird landed near her and she crossed her arms
and swept her heel across the slate in front of her.
Not a kick exactly. A dismissal. And it flew away, of course,
that bird, because it could.

FOUND LOVE POEM

As they were leaving, the blind man
reached for her hand.
The offering of it, a certainty.
Earlier, she had drawn the glass
to his palm and guided his fingers
to a spoon. Then, she pulled some meat
from the bone for him, and shooed
from his plate the flies
he did not know had landed.

TOWN OF MY RETURN

One day I came back. Finally
was the word everyone was thinking.
It was the same season but a different year
and greener than before. I had been
in the far country. I had not died, though
I had tried to. And it was as if everything
had grown around me. Negative space.
Now it was as if there had never been
any unkindness. There had not been doubt.
I had never been afraid. Even now
when I see you as a figment in the air
I am not afraid. And when the purple finches
nested and birthed on the porch where we lived
I was careful. Especially when they came
to resemble us, as everything does for a while.
For instance, they were not startled
if I moved slowly enough in the dark around them.
They stayed but briefly.
And some days I forgot they could amaze me.

TOWN OF THE END OF THE AFFAIR

Though there is some hatred like a bulb
in the heart they undress only once more.
Without speaking and without kissing.

An appalling kind of farewell, neither
cherishing the other any longer.

The rooms empty of small things first—
silverware, books, a mirror on an easel.
Nail by nail from the wall. The radiators off.

Watermark on the ceiling, wind-beaten bluebottle
on its back in the sill. Spider and cricket shell.

The leaving has a fragrance
she will spend her life remembering, trying to
name exactly the last scent. Once beside the cypress

at the edge of the cliff by the sea it was almost
there. And almost again inside a yellow

room inside an air-lit church inside a Greek city.
Again on a market street when a brown-haired boy
walked by with an ice bucket and in a hurry.

It has come to be like this: a desire for precision
and sweetness, truth, fondness, attention,

remembering carefully the one she
starts to forget again, the one—didn't he?—

who must have nearly loved her, must have.

BRIDE TOWN

She wanted to crouch by the koi pond
and show you the wild orange in the water-nest.
Only for you did she want to point out as she would a star
the white moth flitting in the high corn.
It was for you when she cleared a place in the zoysia grass.
And in the flatlands where she was sweeping the flies from the
   animals.
Did you not know the whole world was a mirror for her desire?
She went to the edge. It was indeed her bellowing
you could hear. And you should have done something.

BEFORE THE WAR

We settled in the bones of the other, our bodies dark

houses—moon-gray shadows, witch moths slipping skin,
quiet as dust, and as certain.

It was summer, heavy and thick,

when we turned in the window the box fan around,
the room's air cooler from emptying it out.

It was the one season we were closing in

on a form of God; we felt something of the Seraphs' burn
and well before we knew the ways we would hate and turn

on one another—sharp, elapsed as a choking.

I want what I wanted then: the image of us tethered and fixed,
so permanent may every woman's tiny bow lips

or delicate neck be mine. Her arm, mine, her back in arch,
mine, mine, her sudden flush, her hand, my clutch.

room of the queen's dreams

TO SEE THE QUEEN

Since I was the one who had been ill,
it was she who came to see me.
Everyone wanted a glimpse of her.
The people emerged from their houses toward mine
and with such caution.
They made a visor of their hands.
It was as if they were to be accounted for,
wading the long uphill, little moving triangles
all I could distinguish at first.
But the queen came to see only me and I saw her.
And my life for a while was forgotten
and so repaired.

THE RESCUE

I wake in the middle of the night because of the cold.
The house sinks with winter, shifting before dawn.
The dog shivers in its sleep. The figment was here.
She told a story of a woman eaten by dogs—
her neighbor's—not even wild dogs.
It did not make me afraid of being killed. Instead
I aimed a pistol at the dogs
and it was the pistol in my hand that was so cold,
which is why she left,
which is how I came awake.

ROOM OF SECOND SLEEP

It is happening again
the dream not yet interrupted
but with little time left
the sleeping self
and the real self form a new self
a Liliana
a figment

This is the room in which I learned patience
If she comes (when she came)
it is quiet
and by her silence
I am comforted

When she offers the drink
I know to drink deeply
it is God's Elianna
(He has answered)
I pour her over ice
in a champagne flute

ROOM OF COMINGS AND GOINGS

milky blue June and endless afternoons
the terror of sadness leaving some every day
Liliana returns in different forms

each one immortal   sometimes a bluebird
on a white gutter or the smell of honeysuckle
or gardenia   the contrail over the house
like a seam in the sky

no one asks questions anymore no one
mentions her or how it is
she vanished   and she does vanish
she comes and goes and remains away

until I see the green paint cracking
      as a vein in the wall
and like that the queen is here again

TRAIN DREAM RECOVERY

I was standing on the bridge
so the train would run under

instead of over me
like it did in my terror when

my body was not whole

(a whole body never as miraculous
as the morning after the night

in which it was not)

and today's rescue is but knowing
and knowing without pause

nothing happened
nothing happened here

LILY BRISCOE, PAINTING

This one was of Lily and water rushing through a window.
In this one nothing is ruined and no one goes unnoticed.

Lily writes a letter and there is a kite in an oak tree.
She thinks it a symbol for something.
Then a ghost wind startles the birds to safety.

What could she paint of the glass and survival?

Could you paint, artist-queen, a field day,
a pearly clarity like today's, down to the fine
lines of the silver trout? It is their shone-on pond

that is the pond that comes through the window
of the room. Paint the saving. And the faulty window,

the only mistake. Lily, paint winter. It is December
and the wind sounds like a woman and the skeleton
of the oak tree moves like her body dancing.

ROOM OF HELD BREATH

Before it was drained, the pool was a smooth yard,
shades of blue as the sea an acre deep.
Often did we sisters stage our drowning and by turns
rescue one another, laughing in the well. Other times
we did not speak but swam underwater, a womb
quieting our unquiet minds.
It was the last summer we were young—artless, afloat,
our eyes like opals.
And then the world's beautiful torture began—
the resurface, the sting, the coming
back gasping, mouth-high in love.

ROOM OF THE CURVED SPINES

I read one way to become yourself again
is to repeat the stories so I sit still
and tell once more about the spines.

I tell of the auxiliary room (florescent and bare
as I pictured a prison) in junior high when the girls
stood in a line as a string of beads

and we one by one removed our blouses—
bras, flesh, the popular girls in lace
(I thought, so that is an enviable back).

Vertebra by vertebra we were inspected like pearls
until my sister and I were among the dismissed
and for our mother, a letter:

they are in no danger, not yet, but watch closely.
Before long, things become permanent.
This feels like the end of that story. But then

there is the part I cannot tell, the pale girl
I do not hold correctly in my heart, the girl I did not know
and yet the one I grieve these decades later

knowing she starved herself to death.
I keep an illusion of her skeleton in bed, the obvious spine,
how it was or was not curved and to what end.

I must tell and tell again about the girl;
I try to see her clearly—so clear she disappears—
her spine the line in which we stood as children, her spine

a letter creased, her spine a necklace and each pearl
a choice. That is as much as I can see or tell:
the remains of a girl starved, her beauty a hook.

ROOM OF SLEEPWALKING

I was being drawn
creme and black from the mouth up.

Liliana painted my sadness with a flue-black streak
on the canvas where my brain would be.

I understand now it was she this whole time
mixing colors in the sink; she who polished the silver

with a scarf while I slept,
she I heard humming with joy;

and she, lamp-tanned at the bedside while I writhed,
who told me of a lovely other world: where

everything is a shade of green, where I find my bracelet
in the wheatfield and a red fox in some enormous woods.

She says to me
dear sleepwalker, dreamer, darling sufferer,

next time you will find whatever
you are after. Next time the kitchen is only

a sunny kitchen, the room where my brushes are drying,
and never again the room with the knives.

TIME OF NEED

In the road, a dog. Days dead,
that dog. Liliana was walking beside me awhile
(I am sure) and I was almost not crying but then found

what I was looking for.
She heaved it for me—all of it, the stench, the weight—
in her thin arms until it was too much.

Tired, she dragged the thing by its wasted paws
all the way home. Her dress was stained. This is how

I learned about love. She did not mind at all
the silent, steady distance I placed between us.

SECRET ROOM

In another life I ended myself and in another
I keep not dying; another, I am unlacing the animals,
pulling a rope through the grass, happy

and thoughtless. In yet another, I am my mother
ripping page after page from a magazine saying
this is what I want this is what I want.

Or I am hanging a painting and no one understands
what I say for the nail in my mouth.
In any of the lives there is always the figment

sitting in the living room or up against the walls.
Sometimes she is even with me in my sea-dark bed
and I jerk her around

and ask her questions in some other language,
a language my real self does not know
but that the sadness knows. The language

sounds like banging on an empty box
or on the bottom of a boat moored.

UNDERGROUND ROOM

They packed me in
by the bucketful
and then by the handful
until even my hair
was buried in sand.
As they drank their beers
underneath the umbrella,
my tiny face (a shell)
was almost forgotten.
Though the tide inched forward
and the sand caved tighter,
it was never quite unbearable,
the breathing.
And if the people moved
out of sight, or fell silent too long
all I had to do
was yell, "Someone?" And a voice
would call back, "Yes!"
And it was not yet
a metaphor for anything.

ROOM OF RESIGNATION

I did something she could not forgive.
She did not have enough pity, not even for the sick,
not when I made the bridge inside me collapse.
As I lay at the bottom of the earth, I was worked on
by strangers until I returned.
She was not there though I thought only of her,
of Liliana and her paint brushes as they entered a glass
of rose water to rinse. A harmless gesture,
one I could have made. But the world is for some
a body of water, the surface a membrane to pierce—

WE BECOME WHAT WE BEHOLD

Liliana is a dream each night
like God like my youth

her beauty is a torment

in the dream she is the flute girl
the mill girl
the queen unpinning her crown

and the secret to the sadness
is there bewitching our brains
like gentle animals

the secret is somewhere along the long
gaze of her body I cannot touch

and I go swimming inside her
each night the secret swimming
she is the taste of dewberries

she is the temperature of my delirium see
we are never to be trusted

NONE SUCH AS SHE

The last of her steps descending
I can hear
the silence of Liliana

without her soon
it will be one hour
then thirty years

gone the precision
of her beauty
her humming in the attic

for now between us
the war is ended
a slat of light in a half-length mirror

all that is left of a queen
but for her pillbox hat
and tea-length dress

a memory
of the yellow bodice
I live on in hope

though for her to die inside me
is not what I want
not exactly not if time

is what we have a world of
not if the world
is a bed I have made

acknowledgements

Some of these poems originally appeared (often in altered forms) in the following magazines and journals. I am indebted to the editors of these publications for their attention and support.

The Allegheny Review: "Slow Night Show"
Arts and Academe: "Town of Unspeakable Things"
Blue Mesa Review: "House Fire"
Crazyhorse: "The Figment" (as "Figment"), "Sick Room," "Wolf Town" (as "First House Elegy"), and "Train Dream Recovery"
Four Way Review: "Town of the Beloved"
Greensboro Review: "Room of Comings and Goings" (as "Ambrosia")
Hampden Sydney Poetry Review: "The Queen," "The Sadness," "The Difficult Way"
The Hollins Critic: "One Man Town" (as "Do You Want To?")
Harvard Review: "Late Apology"
Heliotrope: "The Sisters' Incident with the Figment at the Bus Stop, 1985," "Room of Sleepwalking" (as "Dear Sleepwalker")
Louisville Review: "Room of Held Breath" (as "The Sisters Extinguished"), "Town of the End of the Affair"
Meridian: "Town of My Return" (as "The Return")
Mid-American Review: "Time of Need"
Mississippi Review: "Room of Resignation" (as "The Affair")
Pleiades: "The Fever" (as "Fever"), "The Rescue"
Poetry: "To See the Queen"
Poetry East: "Found Love Poem"
Richmond Magazine: "Secret Room"
The Southern Review: "Lily Briscoe, Painting" (as "Letter to the Artist: Mother and Daughter, or, Lily Briscoe, Painting"), "Runaway Bride"
The Sycamore Review: "Town of Small Fields" (as "Spoken For")

I also appreciate the editors of *Poetry* for reprinting both "Time of Need" and "Town of Unspeakable Things" and the editors of *VerseDaily.org* for reprinting "Runaway Bride." I am grateful to *Born Magazine* for reprinting "House Fire" and to Filepe Hefler for his stunning work on the project.

I offer my sincere thanks to Don Share and the Poetry Foundation for a Ruth Lilly Fellowship that allowed me the time and silence to create art; to the Virginia Center for the Creative Arts for its space and beauty; and to the Dorothy Sargent Rosenberg Foundation for its enduring goodwill. For their essential support and generosity of spirit, I am grateful to many people, most especially my parents, Pam and Warren, sisters Erika and Emily, brother-in-law Lars, and my sweet Aunt Patti; also Toy O'Ferrall, Renu Shah, and Jennifer Whitaker, whose talents continue to inspire me; and Eric Shaffer, for his patient heart and unrivaled loyalty.

Thank you to my gifted teachers and mentors, and to the insightful readers of this manuscript: Van Jordan, Stuart Dischell, Julia Johnson, Carrie Brown, Linda Gregg, Richard Dillard, Christine Garren, Lisa Russ Spaar, Kathy Pories, and my dear friends Laura Van Prooyen, Matt Fiander, Madeline Huey, Bob Worrell, Emma Parker, Chace Clay, and the brilliant Laura Pharis. Thank you to Lynchburg College, the University of Mary Washington, my colleagues and students, and to the entire community at the University of North Carolina at Greensboro, especially Jim Clark, Terry Kennedy, Lee Zacharias, Fred and Susan Chappell, Brian Crocker, Anne Wallace, Lydia Howard, Melanie Humpal, Alyson Everhart, and my incomparable Women's Group.

I am indebted to my first and best mentor, Claudia Emerson, for her unflagging belief in and devotion to poetry; to Robert Wrigley for his wisdom and encouragement; and to my beloved friend Michael Parker, whose kindness has been central to my life.

I offer special thanks to Willie Bullock for illuminating the days with joy.

Finally, I dedicate this book—with great respect for the Lexi Rudnitsky Poetry Project and the wonderful people at Persea Books—to Gabriel Fried, with profound and eternal gratitude.